EXPLORE DELHI

by Douglas J. Fehlen

STORY LIBRARY

www.12StoryLibrary.com

Copyright © 2020 by 12-Story Library, Mankato, MN 56002. All rights reserved. No part of this book may be reproduced or utilized in any form or by any means without written permission from the publisher.

12-Story Library is an imprint of Bookstaves.

Photographs ©: Kingsly/Shutterstock.com, cover, 1; diy13/Shutterstock.com, 4; clicksabhi/Shutterstock.com, 5; Marzolino/Shutterstock.com, 6; Elliott & Fry/PD, 7; Subodh Agnihotri/Shutterstock.com, 8; Abhisheklegit/Shutterstock.com, 9; Marcin Mierzejewski/Shutterstock.com, 10; Sandra Foyt/Shutterstock.com, 11; Natalia Deriabina/Shutterstock.com, 11; Avigator Fortuner/Shutterstock.com, 12; NICK MELNICHENKO/Shutterstock.com, 12; Diego Grandi/Shutterstock.com, 13; Capricorn Studio/Shutterstock.com, 13; clicksabhi/Shutterstock.com, 14; paul prescott/Shutterstock.com, 14; travelwild/Shutterstock.com, 15; Sumit.Kumar.99/Shutterstock.com, 16; suronin/Shutterstock.com, 16; JeremyRichards/Shutterstock.com, 17; Stefano Ember/Shutterstock.com, 18; null0/CC2.0, 19; RavinderKanyal/Shutterstock.com, 20; Nicolo' Zangirolami/Shutterstock.com, 21; Curioso/Shutterstock.com, 21; Mahesh M J/Shutterstock.com, 22; promicrostockraw/Shutterstock.com, 22; TK Kurikawa/Shutterstock.com, 23; Sumit.Kumar.99/Shutterstock.com, 23; Yavuz Sariyildiz/Shutterstock.com, 24; Prince9/Shutterstock.com, 24; Morenovel/Shutterstock.com, 25; Snehal Jeevan Pailkar/Shutterstock.com, 26,30; Rakesh Nayar/Shutterstock.com, 26; Jason Garnier/Shutterstock.com, 27; seeyah panwan/Shutterstock.com, 29

ISBN
9781632357236 (hardcover)
9781632358325 (paperback)
9781645820109 (ebook)

Library of Congress Control Number: 2019938657

Printed in the United States of America
September 2019

About the Cover
The Qutub Minar minaret in Delhi is a UNESCO World Heritage Site.

Access free, up-to-date content on this topic plus a full digital version of this book. Scan the QR code on page 31 or use your school's login at 12StoryLibrary.com.

Table of Contents

Hot and Dry Delhi Is on the Yamuna River 4

Its History Includes Many Rulers 6

The Population Is Diverse 8

Delhi Has a Thriving Economy 10

The Architecture Is Old and New 12

Delhi Has a Modern City's Infrastructure 14

Delhi Is a Cultural Center 16

Delhi Loves Sports 18

Visitors Come for Delhi's Sites and People 20

Delhi Offers Great Food and Shopping 22

The City Has Wide Gaps in Wealth 24

Delhi Knows How to Celebrate 26

Fun Facts about Delhi 28

Where in the World? 29

Glossary 30

Read More 31

Index 32

About the Author 32

1
Hot and Dry Delhi Is on the Yamuna River

Delhi is a massive metropolitan city.

Delhi is in north central India. It has two parts. Old Delhi lies to the north. It is the city's historical area. New Delhi is to the south. It has been the capital of India since 1947.

The city is among the largest in India by land area. It is set on the Yamuna River. Two Indian states surround it. Uttar Pradesh lies to the east. Haryana wraps around it to the north, south, and west. Delhi is about 100 miles (161 km) south of the Himalayas. It is edged on the south and west by the Aravalli Range.

Summer is hot in Delhi. The season goes from March through June. Temperatures can rise to over 100 degrees Fahrenheit (37°C). Summer is also very dry. Things change in July. That's when monsoon season begins. Delhi gets most of its rain

A SACRED RIVER UNDER THREAT

The Yamuna River is sacred to India's Hindu population. It is also the most polluted river in India. Factories dump chemicals into it. Parts are covered in toxic foam. Human waste makes the water dangerous. The river is so polluted in Delhi that it is considered a dead waterway. Plants and animals struggle to survive.

from July to September. Totals average 23 inches (600 mm). That is about three-quarters of the city's precipitation for the entire year.

Delhi winters extend from November to March. The weather is usually mild. January has the coldest temperatures. Daily low temps may dip to 45 degrees Fahrenheit (7°C).

573
Land area of Delhi in square miles (1,483 sq km)

- Over 300 square miles (783 sq km) is designated rural.
- The city is divided into 11 districts.
- High ground called the Delhi Ridge extends over 22 miles (35 km) around the city.

Its History Includes Many Rulers

Over the centuries, India has had many capitals. Delhi has been the capital longer than any other city. Its history includes many conflicts. Different groups have held control. Delhi's people are known for rising up to overthrow rulers.

People settled Delhi thousands of years ago. The area has since been destroyed and rebuilt several times. Historians talk about the Seven Cities of Delhi. That is the number of cities believed built on the site from 1100 CE leading up to British rule.

In the 1600s, the British East India Company started trading with India. By the mid-1700s, the company was ruling the country. It even had its own army. In 1858, the British government took over. The people of India fought colonialism. But they were defeated.

At that time, Calcutta (Kolkata) was the capital of India. But the British wanted Delhi to be the capital, so they moved it there in 1911. They chose an area of the city and raised new buildings for state offices. This area of development became known as New Delhi.

Tensions grew between the British government and the people of India. The people did not think they should be controlled by another country.

There have been many conflicts in Delhi's long history.

Mahatma Gandhi in 1931.

In the following decades, they protested British rule. Mahatma Gandhi was an important leader. He led a peaceful resistance. British forces sometimes responded with violence. Other countries condemned Britain's rule. India eventually gained independence in 1947. New Delhi stayed the capital. It has been the political center of India ever since.

TIMELINE

1400 BCE: A city called Indraprastha is believed to have existed on the site of Delhi.

1100 BCE: Raja Dhilu is built, the first recorded reference to Delhi.

1192 CE: Forces from the northwest defeat Prithviraja III and bring Islam to the city.

1803: The British take control of Delhi.

1857: The Indian Mutiny occurs over several months, but the British keep control of the country.

1911: Britain creates a new Indian capital called New Delhi.

1947: India becomes independent.

2001: India's Parliament is attacked by terrorists.

2011: Delhi's Metro begins operation.

70
Area in square miles (180 sq km) of the Delhi Triangle

- It contains the sites of the Seven Cities of Delhi.
- The cities grew in size over time.
- Some say up to 15 cities may have preceded Delhi on this land.

3 The Population Is Diverse

Delhi is India's most populous city. And it is growing quickly. In 2019, there were 29 million people living in and around Delhi. The United Nations estimates that 37.2 million will live there by 2028. It will be the world's largest city by population.

It is already the world's most multicultural city.

Delhi's population is diverse. People have many different ethnic, religious, and cultural backgrounds. The city has been an important trading center in Asia for centuries. Traders from many regions have settled there.

Colonialism has contributed to Delhi's

Delhi is a crowded, yet multicultural, city where people embrace diversity.

People often have to line up to get water from a tanker truck.

diversity. Great Britain ruled India from 1857 to 1947. People from Great Britain still live in the city. After Indian independence, Hindu and Sikh refugees arrived in Delhi. Large numbers of people from other Indian states have moved to the city over the years.

Despite this diversity, people mostly get along with one another. They often embrace others as *Dilliwalas*, or those from "the place of people with big hearts." Still, inequalities are part of life for many in Delhi. Up to half of the city's residents live in slums.

In these areas, millions live without running water. People have to go to the bathroom outdoors. Drinking water and food can be hard to find. The government is trying to address these challenges. But much work remains to be done.

150,000+
Number of homeless people in Delhi

- Thousands of migrants arrive in the city each day from surrounding areas.
- These people are looking for work, but many fail to find employment.
- Migrants often cannot obtain housing and end up living on the streets.

4 Delhi Has a Thriving Economy

Cyber City is considered one of the largest hubs of IT activity in the city.

India has the fastest-growing large economy in the world. Delhi helps drive the country's growth. Its gross domestic product (GDP) rose 12 percent from 2011 to 2019. It is the second richest city in India, after Mumbai.

Financial services are an important part of the Delhi economy. Many banks, investment firms, and insurance companies are found here. These include the Punjab National Bank, with headquarters in New Delhi. They are major contributors to the city's wealth.

The city is a center for information technology (IT) companies as well. Global brands like Google and Microsoft have offices in Delhi. The city government actively helps tech startups get established.

Another priority is manufacturing. Launched in 2014, a "Make in India" campaign is a nationwide effort to boost manufacturing and create new jobs. Many sites in Delhi are focused on food production.

THINK ABOUT IT

What are some of the important industries where you live? What types of companies create the most jobs? Try to find out.

Delhi's service industry is booming. More than 12 million people visit the city each year. Hotels, restaurants, and other hospitality sites employ hundreds of thousands of people. These workers serve locals and visitors alike at Delhi establishments.

2.8 million
Number of foreign tourists visiting Delhi each year

- More than a quarter of India's international visitors arrive in Delhi.
- India is one of the largest countries in the world. Millions of tourists from around India also visit Delhi.
- Visitors are critical to the economy, especially service industries.

Tourism is important to Delhi's service economy.

5
The Architecture Is Old and New

Delhi has many ancient landmarks. Most historic buildings are in Old Delhi to the north. In the south, New Delhi has more modern architecture.

One of the most famous buildings in Delhi is Qutub Minar. Work on the tower began in 1193 CE. More stories were added over time. Today the tower rises 240 feet (73 m) into the air. A mosque at its base is a reminder of the city's Muslim past.

Humayun's Tomb is another historic site. This symmetrical building from 1570 is India's first garden-tomb. More than 150 Mughals are buried there. The Mughals were a family who ruled India from 1526 to 1803. The Red Fort was built in the seventeenth century. It is a symbol of India. Its sandstone walls rise 75 feet (23 m). Visitors tour palaces and gardens inside.

After India gained independence from Britain in 1947, the government wanted India to have a new look. Several modern

The Qutub Minar (left) and Humayun's Tomb (right).

27
Number of "petals" that make up the Lotus Temple

- The temple is a place of worship for the Baha'i faith.
- It opened in 1986.
- As many as 10,000 people visit every day. It is open to all, regardless of religion.

The Lotus Temple is open to all, regardless of religion.

THE TAJ MAHAL

Delhi visitors often travel to nearby Agra to see the Taj Mahal. Its design is based on Humayun's Tomb. Begun in 1632, it took 20,000 workers more than 22 years to build. The mausoleum of white marble is perfectly symmetrical. It is surrounded by a large garden that includes a reflecting pool. The Taj Mahal is one of the new Seven Wonders of the World. It is also a UNESCO World Heritage Site.

structures sprang up in New Delhi. These include the Palika Kendra building and the modernist National Dairy Development Board building. The Lotus Temple is a place of worship. Its petal-like structures rise up over a central hall.

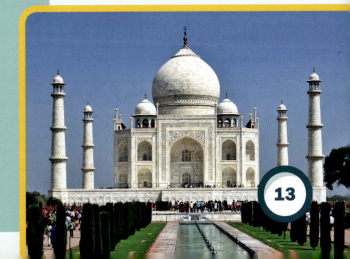

6
Delhi Has a Modern City's Infrastructure

Delhi has a quality transportation network. Trains, buses, and taxis operate throughout the city. More than half of the city's population relies on these services to get around. Visitors also use this transit system.

It can be challenging to travel around Delhi in cars. Roads connect all parts of the city. But traffic is often heavy. Congestion is so bad that exhaust creates dangerous air pollution levels. New roadways are planned to improve traffic flow.

Many people in Delhi enjoy safe drinking water. But others cannot drink from the tap. The city gets much of its water from the Yamuna River. The waterway is heavily polluted in some areas. Factories release chemicals into it. Human waste makes it into the river.

The Indira Gandhi International Airport (IGIA) is the world's entrance to Delhi. People also use it for flying to and from other Indian cities. Nearly 70 million people pass through each year. IGIA is India's busiest airport and the twelfth most traveled airport in the world.

Many people in India do not have access to the internet. But Delhi is an exception. Ninety percent of the population can go online. Internet access is especially important to the many tech workers in the city.

236
Number of Delhi Metro stations

- The system covers 203 miles (327 km).
- Nearly 3 million people travel in its trains each day.
- Many stations feature murals and other works of art.

THINK ABOUT IT

How do people get where they need to go where you live? What could be done to make travel safer and easier?

Delhi Is a Cultural Center

Important museums are found throughout Delhi. The National Museum tells the history of India. Visitors can see items thousands of years old. The museum has pieces from every era of the country's past.

People who love contemporary works visit the National Gallery of Modern Art. It displays creations by Indian artists going back to about 1950. Much of the museum's collection focuses on the impact of Britain's past rule over the country. The National Gandhi Museum is the place to learn about the life and work of Mahatma Gandhi. He led India to independence. Gandhi has inspired many great leaders including Dr. Martin Luther King Jr. and Nelson Mandela.

The performing arts are popular in Delhi. They are celebrated in public festivals year-round. The Summer Theater Festival is one. The National School of Drama puts on well-known plays over several weeks each year. The Popular

This sculpture of Surya, the Hindu god of the Sun, is on display at the National Museum.

Teenage dancers perform in traditional tribal outfits at the India International Center.

INDIA INTERNATIONAL CENTER

Arts and culture events occur all over Delhi. One important location is the India International Center. For more than 50 years, it has been a place where people gather. Some events feature speakers. They talk about government, religion, and culture. The building also hosts dance and theater performances and film screenings.

Theater Festival draws crowds from May through June.

India has the world's largest film industry. Delhi hosts important events celebrating moviemaking in the country. The Habitat Film Festival in May screens dozens of films. The World Classic Movie Festival in June draws fans. This event focuses on the history of cinema.

200,000+
Number of items in the National Museum's collections

- The museum was established in 1949.
- Some of the items on display are more than 5,000 years old.
- The collections are national and global.

Delhi Loves Sports

Delhi residents enjoy sports. Cricket is the most popular. Its importance can be traced to British rule over India. Professional players from Delhi compete against the best teams in India. Tens of thousands of fans cheer on their teams at cricket grounds.

Football, also called soccer, is another popular sport. Like cricket, it was brought to Delhi during the colonial period. Today the Delhi Dynamos compete in the Indian Super League. They play matches in Jawaharlal Nehru Stadium. This site also hosts contests for India's national team.

Individual sports are popular as well. Tennis is one. The Delhi Gymkhana club has grass courts, clay courts, and 14,000 members. Nearly 3,000 people are on the waiting list to join. They might have to wait as long as 37 years. The Delhi Golf Course has 3,000 members. Its wait time is 35 to 40 years.

Cricket is a favorite sport in Delhi.

The Jawaharlal Nehru Stadium is home for the Delhi Dynamos Football Club.

THE ASIAN GAMES

Delhi hosted the first Asian Games in 1951. Fewer than 500 athletes competed. The city hosted the games for a second time in 1982. More than 3,400 athletes competed. Today more than 40 nations participate. Athletes compete in dozens of sports. The Asian Games are the second largest global sporting event. Only the Olympics are bigger.

55,000
Number of cricket fans the Feroz Shah Kotla Ground can hold

- The stadium opened in 1883.
- It has had extensive renovations.
- It is one of the oldest cricket grounds in India.

Swimming is another favorite activity. Many people go to the Pacific Sports Academy for lessons and training. The site features an Olympic-size swimming pool and a fitness center. Dance, skating, and yoga lessons are offered as well.

Visitors Come for Delhi's Sites and People

Delhi is known as a melting pot. People of different backgrounds and beliefs live there together. Many sites display this diversity. These places help make Delhi the most visited city in India.

Parks are great places to see Delhi's unique population. The city has several large green spaces. One is Lodi Garden. It is popular for walks and picnics. Many locals spend time among its gardens and ancient ruins. Sunday afternoon is the best time for people watching.

The Sunder Nursery is another famous park. It has hundreds of types of flowers and trees. The nursery is set on 90 acres (36 hectares). Birds and butterflies fly among the greenery. Visitors also

A WORLD HERITAGE CITY SOMEDAY?

Delhi is an important historical and cultural site. But it has yet to be fully recognized as a World Heritage City. Only the United Nations Educational, Scientific, and Cultural Organization (UNESCO) can grant this status. Delhi has several UNESCO sites. But it has yet to be named a World Heritage City.

The Khari Baoli market in Delhi has been in operation since the 17th century.

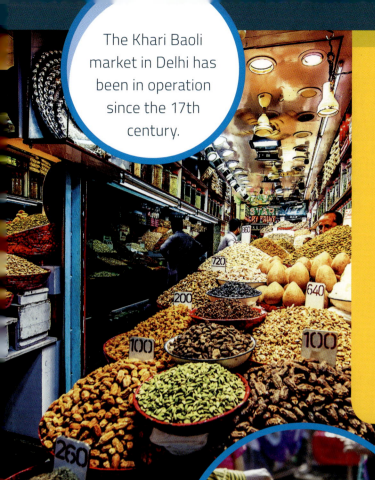

6
Number of major religions represented in Delhi

- Many residents identify as Hindu, Muslim, Sikh, Christian, Buddhist, or Jain.
- People worship at hundreds of religious sites throughout the city.
- Many of these buildings are also popular tourist attractions.

observe the fountains and monuments.

Nature lovers enjoy Delhi's green spaces. But other visitors want different experiences. People enjoy visiting famous buildings. Many are in Old Delhi. Qutub Minar, Humayun's Tomb, and the Red Fort are a few. These sites help tell the story of the city.

Street markets are also popular. Delhi has a spice market that has operated for centuries. Khari Baoli continues to be a favorite spot for buying herbs and spices. Khan Market offers more modern goods. Books, apparel, and household items are sold.

10
Delhi Offers Great Food and Shopping

Chole Bhature is a popular street food.

Delhi is known for its food. Some restaurants serve global dishes. Others offer cuisine from around India. People also enjoy local favorites.

Chole Bhature is one such dish. It includes fried bread, onions, and spicy chickpeas. Many in Delhi eat it for breakfast. Butter chicken is also popular. A spicy cream sauce is poured over chicken.

Some of Delhi's best-known foods are served in the street. Parathas are bread with vegetables and meat stuffed inside. Another popular street food is chaat. Fruits, vegetables, and meats are included in this spicy favorite.

Some of Delhi's best shopping is found in local markets. The Delhi Haat is a large one. Here people sell clothes, crafts, and other goods. Janpath Market is another place to find deals. Clothing and jewelry are popular products. Gaffar Market is known for its electronic goods.

People looking for the latest styles visit many Delhi spots. The DLF Promenade has stores with affordable fashions. The DLF Emporio has costlier goods. Shopping centers like Crescent Mall, City Center, and MGF Metropolitan Mall help make Delhi a shopping destination.

Most people living in Delhi cannot afford to shop or eat at these places. Stores and restaurants are visited only by the wealthiest Delhiites. Visitors from outside the city make up the rest of business at shops and eateries. More than 12 million tourists help support the local economy.

100+
Number of luxury retailers in the DLF Emporio mall

- The site draws Indian and international shoppers.
- Global fashion brands like Louis Vuitton and Armani have shops here.
- Stores also sell watches, jewelry, and other luxury goods.

Great deals can be found at the famous Janpath Market.

11 The City Has Wide Gaps in Wealth

While many live in slums, the city is developing to improve living conditions for the poor.

People in Delhi live close together. The city ranks No. 14 globally in population density. Neighborhoods are often crowded. Shortages of goods can make it hard to survive.

The city has more than 6,000 slums. Almost 2 million people earn less than $17 a month. Most are migrants who came to Delhi hoping to find a better life. Many do not have shelter. Food can be hard to find. Even water is limited. People work long hours and make very little money. Parents have a hard time supporting their children.

Those who are wealthy enjoy a much better life. They live in gated neighborhoods called colonies. They go to restaurants, nightclubs, and other entertainment as other people struggle to stay alive. Organizations in Delhi are trying to create a fairer system. They want to improve the lives of the city's poorest people.

Education is one area of hope. Children in Delhi must attend school

73
Percentage of India's wealth held by the top one percent of its richest people

- Worker incomes rose by two percent over 10 years.
- Over the same period, billionaires became six times richer.
- Gender inequality is part of the problem.

THINK ABOUT IT

Are there wealth gaps where you live? What does your community do to help people who can't afford to meet their basic needs?

from age 6 through 14. Government schools are free and meals are provided. The school year runs from June through April. At some schools, lessons are taught in both Hindi and English. Many Delhi students go on to higher education.

12 Delhi Knows How to Celebrate

People in Delhi enjoy many holidays. Independence Day on August 15 is a major one. This is a time to show pride in India. Parades celebrate the end of British rule. Republic Day on January 26 is another patriotic holiday. It marks the anniversary of the constitution and modern India's birth.

On October 2, people observe the birth of

Along with parades, the President's House is lit with the colors of India's flag to celebrate Republic Day.

19
Number of bank holidays each year in Delhi

- On these days, banks and other places are closed.
- Many people do not have to work on these days.
- Delhi residents observe both national and religious occasions.

26

Mahatma Gandhi. Many consider him to be the father of the country. Gandhi is honored on this day with prayers and songs.

Many other celebrations occur in Delhi. Diwali is a Hindu festival. It marks the victory of good over evil. The event is held in September or October. Buildings are covered in colorful lights. People enjoy fireworks over the city. They also perform rituals and say prayers.

The Delhi International Arts Festival features artworks of all types. Music, poetry, dance, film, and theater are some. Works are on display over several weeks in December. Culinary talent takes center stage in the same month. The Street Food Festival offers foods from a wide variety of vendors.

CELEBRATING MANGOES

Mangoes are important to India. The fruit is a favorite snack. It is also sold to other nations. Delhi's International Mango Festival celebrates the fruit. The event offers hundreds of types of mangoes. They come from growers near and far. Mango-eating contests and magic shows are part of the festival.

Fun Facts about Delhi

- Area: 573 square miles (1,483 sq km).
  Population in 2019: 29 million.

- By population, Delhi is the second largest city in the world. Only Tokyo has more people.

- The city has Asia's largest spice market. Khari Baoli has been open for more than 350 years.

- Delhi's Qutub Minar is the world's tallest brick minaret.

- New Delhi is home to the International Museum of Toilets. Its purpose is to educate people about sanitation.

- Forests cover 20 percent of Delhi's land area. That is 10 times more than in 1997. Environmental efforts have increased forestlands.

- Delhi's public transportation system is made up entirely of vehicles powered by natural gas. These vehicles are better for the environment.

- The official currency used in Delhi is the Indian Rupee. It takes about 70 Indian Rupees to equal one US dollar.

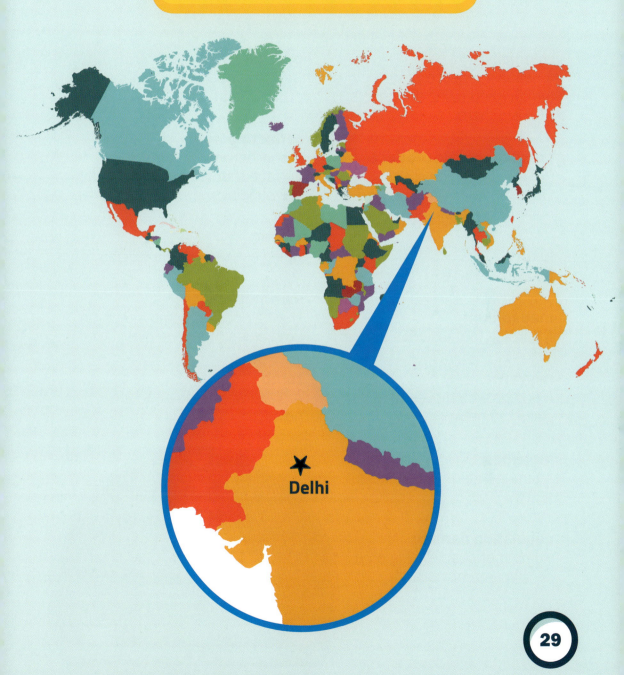

Glossary

colonialism
A nation's practice of taking over territory and ruling the people who live there.

gross domestic product (GDP)
Value of goods and services made within a country.

luxury
Being expensive.

mausoleum
A building that includes tombs.

migrant
A person who moves to another place to find work.

monsoon
A strong wind that brings a lot of rain.

population density
Number of people living on a certain area of land.

precipitation
Rain, snow, and other forms of water that fall to land.

reflecting pool
A shallow pool with a still surface that reflects the surroundings.

sacred
Being connected to a religion.

symmetrical
Having equal size and shape on both sides of a centerline.

tomb
A place where the dead are held.

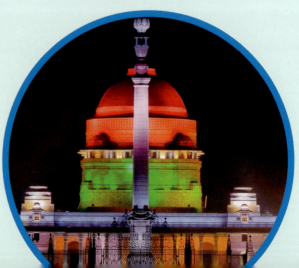

Read More

Roberts, Jack. *A Kid's Guide to India.* Palm Springs, CA: Curious Kids, 2019.

Perkins, Chloe. *Living in… India.* New York: Simon and Schuster, 2016.

Viraraghavan, Chitra. *Delhi Thaatha: A Great Grand Story.* Calcutta, India: Seagull Books, 2018.

Visit 12StoryLibrary.com

Scan the code or use your school's login at **12StoryLibrary.com** for recent updates about this topic and a full digital version of this book. Enjoy free access to:

- Digital ebook
- Breaking news updates
- Live content feeds
- Videos, interactive maps, and graphics
- Additional web resources

Note to educators: Visit 12StoryLibrary.com/register to sign up for free premium website access. Enjoy live content plus a full digital version of every 12-Story Library book you own for every student at your school.

Index

arts, 16-17, 27
Asian Games, 19

British rule, 6-7, 18, 26

diversity, 9, 20

education, 24-25

festivals, 16-17, 27
film industry, 17

Gandhi, Mahatma, 7, 16, 27

historic sites, 12
history, 6-7
holidays, 26

inequalities, 9, 25
Information technology, 10

internet access, 15

Lotus Temple, 13

manufacturing, 10
markets, 21, 22-23
migrants, 9, 24, 30
museums, 16-17

pollution, 5, 14
popular food, 22-23
popular sites, 20-21
population, 8-9, 28, 30
poverty, 24-25

religions, 13, 21
sports, 18-19

Taj Mahal, 13
tourism, 11
transportation, 14-15

wealth, 10, 24-25
weather, 4-5

Yamuna River, 4-5

About the Author

Douglas J. Fehlen is an elementary educator. He is also a longtime editor of books for kids and teens. Douglas lives in Minnesota with his wife, two dutiful dogs, and one curious cat.

READ MORE FROM 12-STORY LIBRARY

Every 12-Story Library Book is available in many fomats. For more information, visit 12StoryLibrary.com